Gloria,
God's bride without
spot or blemish!
Agape
Celia
9/20/15

God Did You Call Me A Toilet?

Are you "Called" by God to Ministry?

Have you not been able to pinpoint your "Call"?

Identify Your Spiritual Gift.

Explore the 5-Fold Ministry Gifts.

Recognize the attributes of 5-Fold Ministers.

Develop skills to support 5-Fold Ministers.

God Did You Call Me A Toilet is the tool you'll enjoy reading. It is informative, innovative and written in a style everyone will understand. Anyone who has ever had questions about their call, 5-Fold Ministers and how they operate in the Body of Christ will definitely find this book a wonderful resource.

God Did You Call Me A Toilet?
Analogy of the 5-Fold Ministry

By

Celia Wilson, MA, OCPS-II

God Did You Call Me A Toilet?
Analogy of the 5-Fold Ministry

By

Celia Wilson, MA, OCPS-II

ISBN: 978-0-615-66940-3
Publisher: Kumenasi Consultants

Unauthorized use, copying and all forms of duplication are prohibited by copyright law unless express written consent is given by the author. Unauthorized use will be prosecuted to the fullest extent of the law.

Scriptures are taken from:

Biblegateway.com

Bible.cc.com

The Open Bible, (NKJV) Thomas Nelson Publishers (c) 1982, 1983, 1985, 1990, 1997, Nashville, TN

US: $12.00

Dedication

To Daphne Burlson:

Sharing the love of Lord with you was and is a blessing. I have been truly enriched as a result of your influence and anointing.

Thank You

Ivan Wilson, for being the first to feed me with milk and then so graciously feeding me meat.

Ruby Denson, for mentoring me in the Word of God, Prayer, the Gifts of the Holy Spirit and for praying your Prophetic Mantel upon me. I wish you were here.

Dan, for respecting the Gift of God inside me enough to call me your spiritual mother. You have no idea how much I praise God for your life.

Table of Contents

1.	Introduction	9
2.	The Living Room Evangelist	23
3.	The Dining Room Apostle	29
4.	The Kitchen Pastor	35
5.	The Bedroom Teacher	55
6.	The Bathroom Prophet	59
7.	Combined Rooms	73
8.	Epilogue	77
9.	Poem: A Chosen Vessel	95

God Did You Call Me A Toilet?

1
Introduction

Ephesians 4:11; It was he who gave some to be apostles, some to be prophets, some to be evangelists, and some to be pastors and teachers.

New International Version (http://niv.scripturetext.com/ephesians/4.

God Did You Call Me A Toilet?

Years ago while living in Rialto, California just before my family and I were going to relocate to Sacramento I was talking on the phone one evening to my sister in Christ, Daphne. We were talking about the Lord and how wonderful He is. Somehow we started to discuss the Gifts of the Spirit, commonly known in Christendom as The 5-Fold Ministry Gifts. We started talking about how the Lord said, "In my Father's house are many mansions, John 14:2.

Then we said houses have rooms. Since we were discussing 5-Fold Ministry Gifts or Offices it made sense that the natural progression for another name for a room would be an office. During our conversation the Lord revealed the purpose of these offices to me using the analogy of rooms in a house.

The Lord had already called me to the Office of Prophet, but this particular night He told me I was a Bathroom. He said until I accepted the fact that I was a Bathroom I wouldn't be able to move spiritually. This was important due to the fact that my feelings were hurt repeatedly because I wanted to be close to my Pastors. While they recognized the Gifts the Lord gave me in one sense by allowing them to flow as the Lord led. On the other hand, I believe only two of them believed I was called to Ministry, even after I told them.

I had even attended ministry school at a local university with my Pastor (before he was my pastor) so I guess I just assumed he knew I was called to ministry, but he never licensed nor ordained me.

During our meetings about this subject he shook his head no as I was telling him I was called to Ministry. He said I should stay home and take care of my children. My husband was in the meeting with us. He was supportive of the ministry the Lord had given me. Did Pastor mean a father with young children is not as needed at home so ministerial work is alright for him or a woman with young children at home isn't or can't be an effective minister? I don't know.

One time the Lord told me to pray for him and his wife to protect them from a satanic attack against their marriage. His wife received the prayer. At least I didn't sense her not receiving it like I did my Pastor. I sensed in my spirit a wall placed up by him signaling that he did not receive the prayer, plus again, he was shaking his head no (unconsciously I think) as I prayed. Eventually, they divorced.

God Did You Call Me A Toilet?

Also, during different ministry activities I sensed I (when I was alone) or my husband and I (when we together) were "a joke" in some ways, which added to my sense of dismay. Now, you all don't know me, but I am funny. I do make people laugh, but I know the difference between someone laughing with me and someone laughing at me. Don't you? This hurt because I really loved them. Years later when we talked about why he hadn't ordained and licensed me he told me he didn't know, he'd just never thought about it.

As Daphne and I talked the Lord revealed the purpose of these offices to me using the analogy of rooms in a house to help me understand why I kept getting my feelings hurt and to understand my purpose and "Place" in the Body of Christ. The Lord said, "You are a Bathroom, You don't belong in the Kitchen. The way you are being treated is not personal. The things that go on in the Bathroom are offensive to Kitchens. You don't want the smells and sights of the Bathroom to linger over into the Kitchen do you." I understood, and replied, "No."

He continued, "When Bathrooms are located close to Kitchens they are separated by some hallway or barrier. You need to back up and stop trying to be close to them. This is necessary because sometimes I may need you to say something to them or I may reveal something to you regarding them and you cannot be their "Friend" as it were because that might influence your decision to obey what I'm leading you to do or say. Your job is to help them. To be effective you must not and should not be in the midst of them." Since then I've learned that there are times when both Offices work together closely as all the Offices are supposed to work together to fulfill God's plans, but initially I needed to understand the separation and function of each Office.

Accepting this spiritual and what would have to be my physical reality was hard, it hurt. However, I had to do as the Lord requested. So I backed up. I prayed. I tried to understand more and more about "My being a toilet in the House of God". All I could see was a big toilet. I did not want that big toilet sitting in the middle of a Kitchen. It wasn't long after this acceptance that the Lord relocated my family to Northern California, far away from my Southern California Pastors. I then understood that the Lord was also preparing me for that move. It would have been so much harder to leave my Pastors without having already put emotional distance between us.

I never doubted that my Southern California Pastors loved me, nor any of the Pastors the Lord sent me to since then. I've been blessed with some wonderful spiritual fathers. My first Pastor after coming back to Cleveland recognized the call on my life. He was going to mentor and use me, but I left that church. I said it was because the music wasn't to my liking and the gifts of the Spirit were not flowing. There was one instrument and they played elevator Christian music. So that was true, but I also left because as a woman I didn't want his wife or anyone to think anything other than Godly endeavors were going on.

It was the same with my next Pastor. He and his wife are wonderful. They loved me and my family, too. He was mentoring me and training me. Then one time as he was taking me home after church we stopped by a drug store and joked that someone might see us and accuse us of something. The scripture Ephesians 3:1 about not letting fornication and other sins be once named among you permeated my spirit. Even though in my situation the term adultery would have been pertinent, I still didn't feel comfortable. I left that church, too.

So I focused on earning my Bachelors in Religious Studies. I didn't want anyone to think anything negatively about him or me, after all "a good name is rather to be chosen than great riches (Proverbs 2:1). Again I backed away and left that church. While seeking the Lord about which church to join next I focused on earning my Masters in Ministry. All along I told My Father, I didn't know why I was going to school specifically, but I loved and trusted Him and I knew He knew what He was going to do with and through me.

I finally joined another church and attended a meeting of teachers called by the Pastor. He told everyone to come up after the meeting to tell him their specialty. I went up and told him I had a Masters in Ministry. He never looked at me.

He said, "You have a Masters". I said, "Yes". He said, "From where?" I said, "Ursuline College". He said, "Hum" and that was it. He never mentioned it again, but he did enroll in school to eventually earn a BA, MA and Ph.D. I even applied for ministerial jobs at the church with no reply. I know he recognized the calling on my life, but for whatever reason he saw no need to ordain or license me.

He often alluded to the fact that women at church whose husband were not active in ministry were not ministerially worthy. If he knew my husband he'd have known that my husband was the first person to really teach me about the Lord, the Bible, Holy Spirit, praying, etc. Wasn't Hosea's wife a prostitute? God didn't care about that. He blessed and used him as a Prophet none the less. I don't know what my Pastor's reasons were. In the end my understanding the reasons are not important. Maybe, all I was supposed to do there was be the catalyst for him to start school.

I am telling you all this for a reason. The reason is God will use you because He called you. Neither you nor other people can totally stop Him, although we do cause delays. Please don't take those rejections personally. I believe many of them are a result of 5-Fold Ministers lacking knowledge, subsequently misunderstanding each other's Offices. If you have been hurt as a result of a misunderstanding like this I pray God heal you right now in Jesus' Name. Lord, heal their spirits, minds, emotions, confidence, ability to trust and minister. Father, by Your Holy Spirit, please let them know You called them and You will work and no one can hinder You. Father, let them know that their work and labor in You is not in vain in the Name of Jesus, Amen.

There are more examples. Another woman I know called to the ministry of Office of Apostle is gifted. She organizes ministries, not necessarily churches, but ministries. She's helped one church get started. They used her blueprint as it were, didn't recognize her contribution for whatever reason. She assists other churches and businesses with their ministerial and operating materials.

Finally, after putting her own ministry on hold she started allowing God to lead her in her own ministry after I finally helped her accept the fact that she had an Apostolic call. However, every time she utilizes her gifts she is told she is not submissive; she is not broken and needs to be.

God is in the saving business and Jesus is in the healing business. He mends broken people. People are in the breaking business. That's some religious misunderstanding which gets turned into religious misrepresentation to manipulate people. It sounds holy, but people are horses to be broken so they can be ridden. God wants us to yield to His Will and to the Holy Spirit. God wants us to know those who are over us in the Lord and He wants us to respect them. Similarly, those over us in the Lord should know us, love us, and respect us, also.

Another Pastor said she was not submitted to her Pastor so how could she be used by God. She has even been told to stop her ministry all together, because her Pastor did not give her permission to do it. Understand God is using her to help people, to bless people. They expect her to stop being a Dining Room, when by no means they can stop being Kitchens. It's who they are. To deny their "Call" would be to deny God's Will for their lives and they will not do it, but they expect this woman, too. It is because they don't understand her call.

Yes, she has growing edges, but where is her Apostolic mentor? I helped her recognize her call, but I am a Teaching Prophetess not an Apostle. There are things I can't teach her, because I don't know them aside from what the Lord reveals to me within this analogy.

Well, what I've come to understand is that these gifts are Body of Christ gifts, not that Pastor's church gifts or this Pastor's churches gifts. They operate as the Lord Wills and we must be obedient to Him. He sends us to "people" in need of our gifts, not just people in church; but people in the World Body because this is the loci of the Body of Christ. God also sends people to us who need our ministry gifts.

Celia Wilson

A man with a deadly brain tumor whom another sister in Christ (educated and called) and I prayed healing for called me his Spiritual Mother the other day. I was touched and overwhelmed with gratitude for the Lord's grace and mercy.

There's another young lady who the Lord sent to me whom I have been mentoring for over 7 years. She is amazing. She has grown so much spiritually. She is training her children up with her new husband in Lord. She is seeking her MA in Pastoral Clinical Counseling. When I met her she was going to major in nursing, but she's recognized her call to ministry. I praise God. These people are the proof of God's Call and anointing, not a license, not ordination.

I and several of my friends have Chaplaincy training (1 unit of Certified Pastoral Education), along with their ministerial degrees. Four C.P.E.'s are the requirement for most Chaplaincy jobs, although we know women who have been hired with 1, but she wasn't African American. One Pastor told me that some members of a group of Chaplains didn't want to open their ranks to accept or admit new Chaplains, or to train them so they could earn their additional C.P.E.'s. That of course is a big WOW! He wanted to advocate for us (I think). I praise God for him.

Nevertheless, I'm sharing all this with you because those called to ministry plan their way, but God directs their steps. There are people who block you and you don't even know they exist. Sometimes it's the work of the Devil to deter you and to try putting your fire out, but sometimes it's God protecting you from mess. Don't blame the vehicles used to try to hinder you. Pray, Pray, and Pray. Then do what God tells you to do.

We are not called to (excuse what I am about to say) to kiss butt or jump through people's imaginary hoops to be accepted or recognized. Nor does anyone have the right to suggest that you are disobeying God because you refuse to be subjected to religious abuse.

Thank God for our Chaplain trainer who continuously reiterated to us that we possess everything within us to do as God instructs. We were seeking validation from particular people when God had already been sending people for us to minister to who were the validations of His Call upon our lives.

Often due to the impediments encountered in churches and other ministerial organizations 5-Fold Ministers are led to Marketplace Ministries. These are ministries the Lord give us to help people outside the local church. All ministries don't have to be inside a church building to be ministry. Often the people who need ministering to are not in church, anyway. Be encouraged and allow the Holy Spirit to develop your ministry as He will.

The Offices of Pastor and Prophet have been revealed to me more than the others because I needed to understand their relationships more. I respect the Office of Pastor. As you'll see they have an awesome responsibility. I've been able to help others understand their Pastors and their Pastors wives so they could pray effectively for them and support them in and with the love of the Lord.

So within these pages I share for how over 30 years the Lord has revealed the functions and place of the 5-Fold Ministry Gifts with me with the hope that 1) you will be blessed because your frustration with being filled with ministry with no ministerial outlet will be alleviated and, 2) you will discover and understand your "Call" from the Lord and, 3) you will develop respect, empathy and compassion for those ministers you encounter over your lifetime, Amen.

Remember this: the **purpose** of all the gifts is to **mature** the saints **so they can work in ministry** so the **Body of Christ is edified** so we become a **unified faith filled, knowledgeable mature church** that **measures up to the stature of Jesus' fullness**. These are ministries the Lord gives us to help the Body of Christ. The Body of Christ is not "your" particular church. Since you are supposed to be matured through preaching, teaching, prophecy and all the other gifts don't you believe at some time you have to actually (1) mature (2) work in your ministry in your church (3) work in ministry outside of church.

Let me see if I understand this. You get saved. You go to church to learn about the Lord. You get fed. You go to church every time the doors are open. You start working in a ministry at church. You tithe and pay your offerings on top of buying everything that is sold. You realize God's call on your life. You tell your Pastor. Nothing happens. You keep working (say) as a Greeter (not your call). Then you die.

Is that what church is to you? Is that what we are supposed to believe? When did you mature? After you matured what were you allowed to do in church? Then if you were led to do work in ministry (because you MATURED) are you supposed to be told to stop or supposed to have your gift ignored? That is not The Church I belong to. Those scenarios are lies and tricks of the Devil.

Look, your first ministry is to your family, period. If you are single live at church. I use to. That is Bible. However, married folks should not live at church. If you are at church all the time when do you clean your house, have sex with your spouse, play with your kids, teach them to read, minister to folks in prisons, in hospitals, or folks in the byways, highways and hedges? When do you meditate on the Word of God and allow God to minister to you? When do you and God love on each other? Is praise and worship the only time you have for this? Wow!

I'm not telling you by any means that you don't have to wait on your ministry. The Bible says you do. God doesn't let novices lead. That is Bible, too. I am telling you that as you are waiting (once you have recognized the Call God has on your life) you are supposed to be trained and mentored in your gift. That training and mentoring can take place in church, conferences, or training events. Your church leaders are not supposed to hold you back or deter you because they are afraid or unlearned in the area of your call. They are supposed to hire people (5-Fold Ministers) who can train and mentor you.

There are mature 5-Fold Ministers in the Body of Christ. They are mature, trained, educated and they love you. Locating them working in church, in their call, should not be hard. At many churches the only ones working are Pastors and those with the Gift of Teaching (not those called to the Office of Teacher). Something is not right with that and it has to change.

Beloved, God is in Charge of your life. Satan can't stop what God has you. If you recognize your Call within these pages, pray and seek God for how you should proceed. Tell your Pastor. Ask God to send you to a mentor. The Gifts and Calling of God are without repentance. Men can't stop God's Will for other's lives. Nor do you have to apologize for the wonderful gifts He chosen to bestow upon you. Rejoice and guard them so that you may walk worthy of them, but use them as He leads you, Amen.

Alright, now before we get into the Rooms let me tell you what I didn't do in the Rooms. I did not mention the T.V., radio, video games or IPods and other electronic devices. Let me tell you why. Those things have the same function regardless of the room in which they are located. Either they inform, entertain or distract. All 5-Fold ministers should be compelling when operating in the Anointing of God. When a minister has to work really hard to deliver a message they usually are not in the Anointing, or they are missing Intercessors, or both.

Here's more regarding the distractions: 5-Fold Ministers have to be vigilant about folks in their ears, because the Devil loves to distract them with stuff that God has nothing to do with. I understand that no one wants someone around them who disagrees with everything they propose. However, they should not have only "YES" folks around them all the time either. They need real praying people who love them around them. Not the real holy people. You know the ones who do no wrong. The super humans that are super holy without sin who are liars and the truth is not in them. No, those people will have 5-Fold Ministers implementing stuff that is so out of the Will of God that the people in the ministry will be devastated.

One day we had this vision of this Minister's office with hearts lying all over the room. I cried. I knew God was crying. This minister had been destroying people's hearts. For this reason all 5-Fold Ministers have to guard

God Did You Call Me A Toilet?

against distractions that will distort the Word and work God desires to flow through them.

2
The Living Room Evangelist

2 Timothy 4: 5; But you, keep your head in all situations, endure hardship, do the work of an evangelist, discharge all the duties of your ministry.

New Living Translation (http://nlt.scripturetext.com/2_timothy/4.htm)
((http://www.newlivingtranslation.com) ©2007)

Studying the life of Timothy will assist you in understanding the work of an Evangelist.

The Living Room is the first room in the house just like the evangelist is usually the first person to introduce people to the Lord. In the Living Room you get a feel for the house. You see if they are modern, country, etc. You learn their style. You ascertain if you can relax in their home or if it formal and you have to kind of remain ridged and staunch. The Evangelist invites people in to the Body of Christ. The Evangelist makes people feel comfortable coming in and is welcoming.

Once in they can rest on the couch or a chair if they choose. They can sit by the fireplace and be warmed. They can then engage in a conversation with the homeowners (God) to learn more about them.

The Evangelist doesn't tell you what your gifts are. Nor does the Evangelist tell you what church to join. All the person called to the Office of Evangelist cares about is ensuring you are saved. The person called to this Office has a passion to get you in the house by telling you all the attributes of the house.

Since the Evangelist travels a lot being located next to the Apostle makes sense. Evangelists need someone to hold them accountable, minster to them and support them. Likewise, their proximity to the Bathroom makes sense. How many Bathrooms do you see in the middle of the Living Room? It is funny in a way, because they both exist to make you feel comfortable, but in TOTALLY different ways. Maybe a better word for how you feel after leaving the Bathroom is relieved. If there's a toilet in the Living Room it's usually because someone is sick, just like when there's a bed in the Living Room to accommodate someone who is ill.

Yes, some Living Rooms have sofa beds so resting, napping, and sleeping are acceptable, because Evangelist need to take care of themselves. What if the Living Room becomes a bedroom and has to accommodate both functions, because there is a lack of space in the house? Well, God is not lacking in space so unless someone else is being helped (ministered to) for a time no one should try to transform the Living Room into a Bedroom.

Some other things to consider in the Living Room are its cleanliness. Is it cluttered, dusty, sparse or just

God Did You Call Me A Toilet?

plain unkempt, dirty? Yes, modern design is clean and sparsely decorated, but it is clean. What if the room is dusty or dirty? Others may be harmed due to the allergens in the room. Does a cluttered room mean the Evangelist is holding on to things, is afraid to let things go, or has some attachment issues?

Is the floor carpeted or does it have wooden floor or marble. Does a hard surface mean the Evangelist is hard or does it mean the Evangelist is easy (not complicated)? I mean easy like the line from the Commodores song "Easy like a Sunday Morning". Do soft surfaces exemplify a gentle Evangelist or one who is cautious? Do busy patterns mean a busy-body Evangelist or one who is just really excited, imbued with a great deal of passion and vision?

Is the room too hot or too cold? If the Living Room temperature is not adjusted to meet everyone's needs some will be uncomfortable. It is the Evangelist's job to see that everyone is comfortable. Does too much heat signify the fire and brimstone message which communicates the "I'm going to scare you into getting saved? You are going to Hell if you don't accept Jesus." The truth is Hell is going to be consumed in the Lake of Fire, so if you go to Hell you will cease to exist. Heat can mean passion, also. Heat can be an indication of zeal. Sometimes the Evangelist might need to regulate the amount of zeal exhibited to others so as not to run them away from the Lord. A Living Room that is too cold could mean the Evangelist has a passion problem. Is the Evangelist burnt out?

See, these are the times when the Apostle's Ministry would come in to offer support and counsel. The Evangelist needs to be ministered to by the Apostle, but if we (The Body of Christ) won't acknowledge their ministerial call how many Evangelists and lost souls are negatively impacted as a result of our inaction or incorrect action? These questions are reasons we must not judge our leaders. They are reasons why they must examine themselves. The Holy Spirit knows what is in the spirit of each of us. He knows our motivations. It is because He knows our motivations that He has given us the 5-Fold Ministry Gifts to work together, to strengthen each other, to pray for one another, to cover one another, and to supplement each other's weaknesses. Bottom line: We NEED each other.

God Did You Call Me A Toilet?

Notes

3
The Dining Room Apostle

Mark 6:30; The apostles returned to Jesus from their ministry tour and told him all they had done and taught.

New Living Translation (http://nlt.scripturetext.com/mark/6.htm)
((http://www.newlivingtranslation.com) ©2007)

Studying what the Apostles did before the time of the scenario in the above scripture will provide a picture of the job of Apostles, as will the life of Paul.

The Dining Room is where people hold formal dinners, so people are fed. It is also a place where some families conduct their family meetings, hold family game night, and paid their bills. It is a place where special occasions are celebrated like Thanksgiving Dinner. These are facets of the Apostle's Ministry. They organize churches, set up ministries, and feed people. They are rarely Pastors who stay in one place and feed flocks, but they do set the table, and prepare a place for people to be fed. Apostles conduct the formal business of the church.

The fact that Apostles don't prepare food, but are responsible for serving it speaks to their responsibility to make sure the meals are safe or adequate. Hence, they return the meals that are spoiled, incorrect, along with rejecting plates and glasses that are dirty, etc. This also reinforces the close relationship between the Apostle and Pastor. Apostles hold Pastors accountable for what they prepare and how they deliver it, which is why today the second type of Apostle is a mature seasoned Pastor promoted to the Office of Apostle; the first is a person "Called" to the Office right out of the gate.

The third type of person with an Apostolic call is the one many Pastors have trouble accepting assistance from (like the lady I mentioned in the Introduction). They have an eye for detail, organization, and are visionaries. They are bold decisive leaders. They are excellent at place settings. They know who should be seated where at the table. At some dinner parties or holiday events if you seat the wrong people next to each other the entire event can be ruined; eye rolling turns to arguments; which turn into fights; which can lead to people being totally alienated or even murdered. They know what to use to best clean the silver so the message is not tarnished. Many of them will probably never be Pastors because their skill set can be intimidating to Pastors. However, you can see how vital this ministry is. Reluctantly, many of the third type of Apostle can be found heading mission focused organizations, not in church.

The same aspects of the Living Room being the correct temperature and clean or cluttered apply in the Dining Room, also. However, the implications are somewhat different. If the Dining Room is dirty what the Apostle Ministers to the other 5-Fold minsters will be tainted. If the Dining Room is cluttered the Apostle won't be able to see the details of Church administration clearly, and will make, or suggest inappropriate, or incorrect policies and/or procedures. If the temperature is too hot the Apostle will put too much pressure (undo pressure) on the other 5-Fold Ministers or the congregations they oversee. If the temperature is too cold they won't be able convey life, love, and empowerment to the aforementioned.

Is the floor easy to clean like wood or is it stained like a carpet? Is the Apostle staying before the Lord, or bogged down by guilt which Jesus died to alleviate us from? Now there are two parts to this, but the key thing to remember is that God knew we would make mistakes; that we would sin so Jesus came to cover our sins (past, present and future). If 5-Fold Ministers have stains, trying to cover them with flower pots or statues can cause someone to stub their toe or trip. It's what I call the Jimmy Swaggert Syndrome. I'm a minister with an issue, but I can't tell anyone, because I'll be judged harshly. No one will understand. I don't have anyone in the Body of Christ I can go to, to trust to help me. Trying to cover up the marks can damage the ministry. Having the misguided assumption that 5-Fold Ministers are sinless is wrong. It can breed a psyche of pride and arrogance. More importantly it will cost the Apostle integrity, honor, respect, and the trust of those depending on this ministry. So where is the stain remover stored, in the Kitchen or Bathroom? We NEED each other.

The second part of this "Stain" issue is everyone has stains. We are human, Praise God. We don't have to spend time trying to cover up our stains. We have

JESUS. Guess what? Jesus covers our stains. PRAISE GOD!!! That's right; every time either we or someone else drops something on our carpet Jesus' Blood covers it. It becomes a brand new carpet.

What the Apostle and other 5-Fold Ministers have to remember to do is immediately take the stains caused by others whom we minister to directly to the Lord. We can't hold on to them. They are not ours, Amen. Consistently trying to deal with, actually handle, or hold on to them is too awesome a task for mere mortals. We have to become experts at calling on the ultimate Stain Remover, Jesus. Sometimes, we call a carpet repairman or purchase a new carpet, altogether. Doesn't that sound like Jesus? Praise God!

This is important because the Apostle ministers to ministers, especially. Some might think the Dining Room is set apart far above the messes the Kitchen and Bathroom has to deal with. However, we must be cognizant of the fact that people eat in the Dining Room. What if they get sick a stomach illness? Do they not run to the Bathroom? Yes, so Dining Rooms, Apostles need Prophets. What if after throwing up the person still feels ill, do they not go lay down in the Bedroom? Yes, Apostles need Teachers. In certain homes we might take the person to the Living Room and have them put their feet up in that big comfy recliner until they feel better. So Apostles need the Living Room, Evangelist, as well.

5-Fold Ministers are not along. We are connected for a reason. We are supernaturally equipped to minister to one another, the other members of the Body of Christ, and the lost, Amen. We have to remember this. We have to acknowledge this. We have to find a way to ensure the atmosphere within the Body of Christ is welcoming (not condemning or judgmental) to others. This way they will come to us if they (when they) need to, so we don't have 5-Fold Ministers dead in hotels because they were afraid to tell us an illness was threatening them, or a host of elicit sexual partners parade through the media recounting our sexual misdeeds, or again we watch as our 5-Fold Ministers are handcuffed, and led away to jail. Before an issue reaches these extremes we should have someone, other 5-Fold Ministers, we can approach as soon the enemy places that thought in our minds, or our lust, pride of life, or illness, eventually, leads us to respond in the affirmative to that thing. It really is a matter of life or death, Amen.

4
The Kitchen Pastor

Jeremiah 3:15; And I will give you pastors according to mine heart, which shall feed you with knowledge and understanding.

King James Bible (Cambridge Ed.) (http://kingjbible.com/jeremiah/3.htm)

Acts 20:28, Keep watch over yourselves and all the flock of which the Holy Spirit has made you overseers. Be shepherds of the church of God, which he bought with his own blood.

God Did You Call Me A Toilet?

The Kitchen is representative of the Office of the Pastor. The Kitchen has to always be clean. The Pastor's job is to pass on knowledge of the Word of God, Good News of Jesus Christ, and The Word of Faith; they're all the same. They are supposed to feed some with milk and some with meat. They are supposed to know the difference. Their job (like all the 5-Fold Ministers) is to mature the Body of Christ, the people God has entrusted to their care.

The Kitchen contains food everyone in the family enjoys eating. In the same way Pastors feed their flocks.

They have to feed more than one person at a time and prepare the meals according to each person's taste. Hence, they have to be accessible to people at all times. Completing homework, paying bills and socializing also occurs in the Kitchen. Pastors teach us how to be socially correct Christians and handle or operate within the business of the church.

There is so much to cover here due to the unique nuances of the Office. I hope I do it justice. There is the specialty of the chef versus the specialty of The House, the cleanliness of the Kitchen, the color of the decor, the readiness of supplies, the prep time, the water flow and the pipes, and temperature. Therefore, I think the best way to approach The Kitchen is to explore each area separately.

The specialty of the chef versus the specialty of The House: Some families prefer Mexican food, or Italian cuisine, or vegetarian fare, etc. Within each of these families the chef might have a specialty such as tamales, lasagna, or 3 bean salad. Likewise, God is concerned about the lost being saved, the saved loving and serving Him, and their efforts and ability to grow in faith, grace and mercy. He cares about His children loving each other and being healed. He is concerned about the Holy Spirit's work in our lives and the visibility, vitality, and virtuosity of the Fruit of the Spirit in our lives. As the owner of the homes concerns are focused on keeping his/her family healthy and safe. God is concerned about these things, because He wants His family to mature for the work of the ministry so that His family is edified.

Some Pastors or Kitchens in God's House have specialties of their own. Some Pastors focus their ministries on faith, others on prosperity, still others on saving souls, others still on grace, and so on. This specializing is fine as long as all the areas God is concerned with are addressed properly and equally. However, problems arise when these Pastors focus more on their specialty to the determent of what God desires.

For instance, if a Pastor focuses on prosperity with the hope that the congregation's prospering will prosper the Pastor. This drive to prosper can overtake Pastors and cloud their judgment. These Pastors can begin to worship "the tools and benefits" of prosperity more than God. They can also begin to focus so much on saving souls that they begin to ignore addressing those things that are necessary for all the baby Christians to mature into fully functioning ministers. The Pastor can focus so much on service and neglect love. What is service without love, without the love of God for everyone? If maturing the people of God is not the purpose of their church why do Pastors have churches or pastor in the first place?

I remember one church we attended was called the gas station because most of the people who joined were already saved. It seemed as if they just joined to be filled up because once they were filled they left. At least this Pastor blessed them before they left.

Some Pastors seem to take it as a personal affront either neglecting or refusing to bless 5-Fold Ministers who leave their churches. When people have eaten and are satisfied they do 4 four things. 1) They stuff themselves, overeat which leads to stomach aches or throwing up. In Ministry that is messy either way. 2) They get up to go do something, which for 5-Fold Ministers is working in their ministerial call. If the Pastor of their church doesn't provide opportunities for them to do so, they leave or start working out of their area in church which causes disorder in the church. 3) They go somewhere to sit down. How effective is a ministry with all their gifted people and 5-Fold Ministers (except the Pastor) of the Church sitting down? 4) They go somewhere to go to sleep. The implications for ministry with this choice are sad. How many of my old heads remember that song "Nothing Comes to Sleepers but a Dream"? Wow!

If God gives a 5-Fold Minister a dream or visions of actually ministering in their call and they (for whatever reason) choose to remain at a church where they are not allowed to fulfill God's Divine call on their lives, that is sad. The entire array of wonderful things God wants to do with and through them lies asleep inside them in the church. He'll use them everywhere else, though. That is sad. It is fitting, appropriate, and respectful when Pastors graciously pray for and bless the 5-Fold Ministers who leave their churches, when either they are called to go somewhere else or the Pastor chooses not to use them.

Another church focused on saving souls. The Pastor probably had a combined Pastor/Evangelist Call (See Chapter 8). I say the focus was on saving souls for 2 reasons. The Pastor said it and once people got saved they left to find a place to mature so they could pursue their spiritual callings.

In the short term I can see how having a specialty is alright. My question is about the long term implications of specializing. The question about specializing does not come from the diversity of the Pastor's Gift, because that is Biblical. My question addresses who are the Pastor's using to facilitate their specialty. Who are their sous chefs, as it were? Babies can't teach, nurture, mentor, and train other babies.

Are Pastors making their determinations about who serves based on outward appearances (like what kind of car does someone drive, or what brand of clothing do they wear, where do they live, are they employed, if so where, in what positions)? Does the Pastor focused on prosperity say, "That person is poor and not prospering so they are not equipped to work here? That person doesn't even have money to tithe to my church."

Answer these questions. What if that person spent hours volunteering at the hospital praying for people while they attended school? What if that person had a powerful healing anointing? What if that person was the co-owner of a business that closed due to the economy and was not eligible for unemployment? Would you overlook and deem this person as "not prospering" denying them the opportunity to bless the members of your congregation? Things like this happen every day. Pastors have to ensure it doesn't, which leads to the next topic.

The cleanliness of the Kitchen: Have you ever been in a filthy kitchen? If so, did you want to eat there? Research shows that people can become ill, even die, from dirty Kitchen and contaminated food. These are real practical facts. Similarly, Pastors are supposed to stay prayed up and free from mess (dirt), because just like in a Kitchen people can become spiritually, emotionally, and physically ill, and die. It is the same with Bathrooms. The difficult part of this is a lot of the dirt, crumbs, and messes left and found in the Kitchen are not a result of the Pastor.

Remember, the Kitchen is always open to all members of the family. Kids come in, make messes, and leave them. You know they drop jelly on the floor or they spill juice. (I have to tell you this: I was reading this book to a friend over the phone. When I got to the above sentence she said just as I read that her husband asked which of the kids dropped jelly on the floor. He told them to clean it up). The teenagers cook something and leave the dishes. There are times when maybe the Pastor tosses something into the trash can, but actually it falls behind it without the Pastor noticing. Later the ant covered food debris is discovered, but by then it is trash day.

What's the point? Pastors have to be vigilant. They not only have to clean up after themselves, but after everyone in the house. The thing is it is not just their job. Apostles are supposed to help them. Prophets are supposed to help them. Intercessors and other Gifts in the Body of Christ are supposed to help them. After all doesn't the Pastor have to sleep or rest sometime? Is the cook in your home awake 24/7? Have you ever heard a person say, "I don't allow anyone in my kitchen?" Well, this mindset is extremely detrimental to the Body of Christ. Pastors are not alone. They do have to allow other 5-Fold Minsters and Gifts in.

The color of the décor: What does the color of the décor have to do with the Office of the Pastor? Scientifically certain colors are more conducive to stimulating the desire to eat, just as certain colors are more conducive to sexual arousal in the Bedroom. Also, colors impact the presentation of the food on the plate. Watch the Food Channel. If someone just slops some food on a plate for you to eat, how do you feel about eating that food?

Some Pastors color their ministries with Evangelism, others are family focused, some are focused on Missionary endeavors, some are focused on

God Did You Call Me A Toilet?

building people's faith, or educating people on the history of the church and the bible. There are probably as many ways Pastors can color their ministries as there are colors to choose to paint a kitchen.

So how do the Pastors "color" their ministries? I have 3 examples. Some ministries are perceived as elitist. I've heard people say they don't want to attend certain churches because the members are bourgeois.

Then there are Pastors who color their messages with doubt. I've heard prayers like: Lord, we don't know what your will is so have your way with Sis. Susie, and if you take her home, Lord, we know she will be in a better place. Wow! The Bible says we are to prosper and be in health, even as our soul (mind) prospers. So why doesn't this Pastor know the Will of God? The enemy comes to steal (life and liberty, peace and joy, etc.), kill (people, dreams, faith) and destroy (families, lives).

The Pastor who colors his ministry with positivity is a good example. There's a television Pastor who has been criticized because he doesn't preach. He admonishes his congregation to think positively, to speak the Word of God, to look forward and ahead, to expect good things, and to believe that they are blessed. He probably has the Gift of Exhortation which you'll read about in Chapter 9.

Pastor's color their ministries or messages according to their personal preferences, skill sets, education, and their particular calling. The color becomes a problem only when it causes harm to the members of their congregations.

Using their messages to further a "bully pulpit" that causes embarrassment to people is abusive and damaging, especially when others know who the topic of the sermon is. This is an example of how the manner in which Pastor's colors their messages impacts their congregation.

The readiness of supplies: The pantry, cabinets, and refrigerator are supposed to be stocked with enough food and supplies to feed the family. Food costs money. I cannot for the life of me understand why Pastors have to work two jobs. All Pastors want to do is preach. They don't do what they do for the money, not all of them anyway. Their salaries should be large enough for them to take care of their families. They should also be provided insurance (home, auto, medical, professional liability). How would you like your surgeon to work 2 jobs or your OB-GYN Doctor?

Well, Pastors are responsible for our spiritual well-being. This also includes our psychological and psycho-social, and socio-economic, and familial relationships. Their children and spouses should be provided scholarships to college, as should the Pastors. Pastors deserve to be well compensated for the major roles they have in our lives. They dedicate their lives to our families. They are there for the births (spiritual and natural), graduations and deaths.

On top of all that Pastors have to hire staff, ensure our churches and grounds are maintained, train employees and volunteer staff along with making themselves available when members of their congregations need them. Today, there aren't that many Pastors who visit the sick and shut-in or members in prison, but there are some who still do. These men and women deserve to be paid for their service. Their professions are honorable and much needed. Paying them enough to actually live on, with a little more to relax and enjoy life is the least we can do for them.

The Bible even encourages us to provide for them financially because we receive spiritual nourishment and nurturing from them. If we followed these biblical principles our Pastors could devote the amount of time needed to adequately pray, study, worship, and take care of themselves; all while pursuing ministerial functions full-time. Our churches could be open during the day for our children, teens, seniors, and the lost. Churches being open on Sunday (Saturday for Seventh Day Adventist) and Wednesday or Thursday is not enough, especially when there are 5 churches on every block.

We pay for everything else we want. I refuse to name all the things on which we spend exorbitant amounts of money. Beauticians live better than some Pastors, because we sure spend money on our hair. I'm not mad at all those who make us look beautiful. They are needed, too. What I'm saying is our Pastors deserve to be well compensated, also, even if they don't ask. I mean how important is our spiritual, and yes, sometimes our physical wellbeing compared to everything else on which we find to spend our money. If you think I'm making this up read Matthew 10:10; I Tim. 5:17-18; Galatians 6:6; and I Corinthians 9:9-14.

Look at the example of the Philippians who took care of Paul financially with more than enough. Giving to our Pastors is a ministry, if we give because we want to. When we give because we are pressured to give or out of a felt obligation the gift is not from the heart, anyway. Remember, *2 Corinthians 9:7; Every man according as HE purposeth in his heart, so let him give; not grudgingly, or of necessity; for God loves a cheerful giver.* Give because you are happy you have your Pastor. When you give a little you get a little, when you give a lot you get a lot. It's just like with taxes. I'm laughing. Verse 12 informs us that the administration of this service supplies the want of the saints (the poor). Here are 2 things about the poor 1) There shouldn't be any poor Pastors and 2) Pastors are included in the saints that scripture is addressing.

We didn't have to give anything other than our hearts to receive salvation. We don't have to give money to receive Healing. Jesus paid for our healing, Praise God! We are already blessed by God. Amen. We are alive. I believe the Philippians honored God in ministering to Paul. Therefore, I believe we, (including our communities) would also honor God by choosing to follow their wonderful example.

Philippians 4:16-19 (ESV) Biblegateway.com

6 Even in Thessalonica you sent me help for my needs once and again. 17 Not that I seek the gift, but I seek the fruit that increases to your credit. 18 I have received full payment, and more. I am well supplied, having received from Epaphroditus the gifts you sent, a fragrant offering, a sacrifice acceptable and pleasing to God. 19 And my God will supply every need of yours according to his riches in glory in Christ Jesus.

The point is some people complain about everything Pastors and their families do. They critique their sermons and their families. They begrudge successful Pastors, while demonizing those whose humanity gets the better of them. Yes, some Pastors delve into criminal enterprises, but the majority of them don't. They deserve to be paid a more than sufficient salary for their work. These men and women are "Called" by God to Ministry. They love what they do. Many do not ever complain about their compensation; bless their hearts, this leads right to the next area.

The prep time: The time and manner in which meals are prepared directly impacts the final product. The same is true of how much time and how Pastors prepare for their services. They have to spend time praying, preparing sermons, studying all manner of biblical, social, cultural, familial, and historical data. Some have to prepare to counsel people. Just think about all the spirits they have to deal with. Think about how consistently folks touch them, hug them, all clamoring for their attention. Don't you think they deserve to be well compensated financially for all this? It takes just as much money for a minister to conduct the everyday activities of life as it does everyone else.

Pastors have to be careful not to think they have arrived spiritually. Acquiring an attitude that "I've Arrive" "I know all there is about the Bible" is counterproductive. God can always provide new revelations. So having our Pastors study to acquire even more practical ways in which we can apply scripture and biblical principles to our lives is very important to us.

They also have to be careful to not overwork themselves. Believe it or not, it is possible for a Pastor to work so much in the church that they actually don't have time to pray, meditate on the Word of God, or study.

The water flow and the pipes: The Kitchen and the Bathroom (in most homes) are the only rooms with sinks and faucets. Some Dining Rooms have wet bars. This means some Apostles have an extra strong anointing; probably to lead Pastorally or Prophetically.

I apologize for neglecting to mention that all the rooms have anointing represented by their lights. Some have dimmers which mean the Holy Spirit has a diminished capacity in that room. Some lights are really bright, which lets us know the Holy Spirit has an important role in that room. Some rooms have a lot of lighting, like a lot of lamps or recessed lighting. This means the person holding that office relies on the Holy Spirit a great deal.

Trust and believe, lights out in a room (or minister) all the time or one missing lighting (illumination), is a room you definitely don't want to enter into to receive ministry. No one's lights should be out all the time. However, the Lord just revealed that all of us have periods of darkness. Yes, we all face our dark nights. It is at these times that we need each other. Praise God! It is at these times that someone should be available to bring a candle into the room, Amen. It is at these times like these that other 5-Fold Ministers can provide support or additional lighting, as it were. 5-Fold Ministers can you hear what the Holy Spirit is saying? Gifts in the Body of Christ can you hear what the Holy Spirit is saying? Are we prepared and willing to aid our brothers or sisters when their lights are fading? Shouldn't we notice problems with our own and other's anointing long before the lights go out?

Alright, back to the water flow and pipes in the Kitchen. Yes, the water is indicative of God's anointing. Kitchens and Bathrooms have lights (anointing) so why do they have more anointing in the water? It's because of the pipes. The ability to clean and remove waste is significant. The garbage disposal in the sink, the dishwasher, and the refrigerator with the water and ice dispenser is representative of the versatility of the anointing on Pastors.

This is really cool. Pastors are gifted at imparting their anointing to others (the water dispenser in the refrigerator door). Their anointing can numb us to pain (the ice dispenser). You know when you've hurt your leg the doctor tells you to put some ice on it. It's the same with this type of Pastoral anointing. They have the power to heal with their words and with the anointing that flows through their hands. Plus, they can store ice so it's available whenever we need it. Thank God!

They can take the residue, the left over aspects of our psyche (personality, feelings, thinking, etc.) that have been damaged and dispose of it in the garbage disposal. That is an amazing feature. Praise God!

The water in the dishwasher speaks to Pastors ability to prepare us for service. Dishes, pots and pans, glasses, cups, silverware are all used to prepare and/or serve food. Pastors have the ability to discern who is a pot, a pan, a cup, etc. They also have the skills to discern how much and what goes into each item (person). Remember, not all Kitchens have dishwashers. What does that mean? Some Pastors have a more distinctive anointing in this area than others. Those who don't need to rely on the other 5-Fold Ministers for this.

However, the water in the dishwasher is also necessary because Pastors have the ability, and must utilize this ability, to remove the residue of our "stuff" off of them. Have you ever been served food on a dirty plate? You refuse to eat it, right? You do the same with sermons or portions of sermons that are incorrect or that are served improperly. For instance, if the Pastor is angry over a personal matter, or if something else is negatively impacting the Pastor's ability to preach. It's the same with glasses that are stained with spots or dishwashing liquid residue. The only thing is a baby

Christian might not possess the knowledge or the skill to reject milk served in a dirty bottle, Amen. So Pastor's dishwasher skills are twofold, cleansing residue off of their congregants and themselves.

Finally, we get to the sink. Of course, if there is no dishwasher the Pastor has to and will clean the dishes in the sink. This Pastor's anointing is different from the Pastor with the dishwasher; with the dishwasher you just press the buttons are everything operates automatically. The ability to manually regulate the flow and temperature of the water is unique. That is why they flow so well with the Minister of Music. The Minister of Music has a unique gift enabling them to discern what, when, how, and why to play certain songs in a particular manner, just as the Pastor has the spiritual sensitivity to follow the flow of the Holy Spirit. Should Praise and Worship be extended? Should prayer be extended? Should a certain topic be expounded upon to a greater degree? Pastors can discern these things.

The Pastor's skill of holding water in the sink is also unique and shared by the Bathroom. Wow! Have you ever attended a service where the anointing was so strong it seemed as if you could touch it or see it? That was your Pastor's anointing. This anointing allows them to lay hands on people. Have you been in a service when the Pastor laid hands on someone and they fell under the Power of the Holy Spirit? That was the Pastor's anointing. It is like a concentrated anointing.

If the sink has one of retractable hoses that people use to spray food or wash their hair with, that is characteristic of another special attribute. This is a localized distributive anointing. Have you ever been in a service when a Pastor called out a certain person (and spoke to their specific circumstance) without having prior

God Did You Call Me A Toilet?

knowledge of the situation? Oh, I see this Pastor has a strong anointing in the Gift of the Word of Knowledge. Praise God!

What happens when the sink is clogged? Well, we know that this is directly related to the anointing. It is not flowing in to the Kitchen. It is not leaving the Kitchen. What does dirty water stuck in the sink represent? It represents a foul spirit that needs to be healed by God. Yes, it can happen.

Doesn't the lack of flowing water affect the garbage disposal? Have you ever smelled the fowl order that emanates from a garbage disposal crammed with old food? Whew! This Pastor is preaching messages that are wrong, old, or the same over and over. If the water is not flowing the Pastor's ability to follow the leading of the Holy Spirit in preparing sermons, praying, healing, preaching, and making decisions that impact the ministry is impeded. The Pastor won't be able to cast out the Devil either, so every evil work will be present in the congregation.

Temperature: The refrigerator has to be the correct temperature to ensure the food is safe to eat. This speaks to the need for Pastors to take care of themselves. If they are stressed, worried, sick, tired, angry, etc. it will affect their ability to prepare and deliver their sermons. Is the light in the refrigerator out, which is indicative of a Pastor who has stopped praying privately?

They also take the temperature of their congregations to ascertain what topics to preach. In the 60's the temperature of congregations was hot. Today, I really wonder if our congregations are warm enough. Why aren't we sweating with ministry to save our kids and our families? Why aren't we sweating to find creative ways to improve the economic situations of families? Corporate prayer is powerful. It's miraculous when mixed with corporate action.

There's another way Pastors take the temperature of their congregations, spiritually. They are equipped to sense when someone is hurting, when someone is facing a particular challenge, and when they need to preach on a particular subject. They can sense when evil is about and when the Holy Spirit changes their (the Pastor's) agenda.

Then what about the temperature of the Pastors spirit, which the stove would represent? Is the Pastor on fire for the Lord or has the burner gone out. Is the Pastor lackadaisical, while everyone is waiting for the water on the stove to boil? Is the Pastor listening to the Holy Spirit or is there a leak in the gas pipe? Are the Pastors sick or are they being tormented with some habit? Remember, they are human. They can be afflicted with Depression, Addiction, etc. Are they harboring some resentment, which would be represented by something burning in an overheated oven?

◇ ◇ ◇ ◇ ◇ ◇ ◇

Here's a note about Pastor's spouses, especially Pastor's wives. Since Pastors jobs are so important their spouses are, too. Pastor's spouses have a tremendous responsibility. They are supposed to love everyone, be hospitable and caring, as their families are exposed to everyone all the time. They aren't supposed to get tired, want privacy, or have a bad day. They have to be "on" all the time and are expected to smile all the time. They and their families are constantly judged by members of the congregation and community. What are they wearing, what are they saying, where are they going, what are they buying, who are their friends, etc.?

Speaking of friends, that's a big area. Who really wants to be their true friends? Some people want to be their "friend" for the prestige, just to say I'm her friend. They want to drop their names in "Church" circles. Some want to be their "friend" for access so they can say I was at their house. Some want access to find dirt, imperfections they can spread to others.

I remember one time a new couple joined our church. They were well educated, lived in a new home, had affluent jobs and tithed regularly. The wife invited some other female leaders of the church and me to her home after church a few times. I went, thinking it would be fun. Maybe, the second time we met she began to say she noticed things about our Pastor's wife and she began to point out her flaws. I immediately sensed a foul spirit. I said something to stop her and never went back to that house again.

There was another time when this female pastor's assistant/best friend and I were talking outside the church one evening. I gather they had been having some problems, because she said, "I know things, I could bring this church down if I wanted to." I told her she didn't want to do that. I told her they were friends and she should respect their friendship. I told her that her place was God given and doing anything to harm her Pastors would harm her instead. She remained that female Pastor's loyal friend and assistant long after I'd left that church. She was even ordained and licensed by them.

Pastor's and their spouses have to be so careful about who they allow to really get close to them. There are some who try that have ulterior motives. Some people befriend them because they do seek a position in the church. Those that do are power mongers and end up wreaking havoc in churches. Then there are those who want to befriend Pastor's wives because they want access to their husband's. That's right the Pastor's groupies. I guess female Pastors have male groupies. I don't know since I've never witnessed this.

Pastor's spouses vary in temperament, education, gifts, and personality. They are HUMAN beings. They make mistakes. They are not perfect. If they are called to an Office the same things from this book that apply to that Office apply to that spouse. For those who are not called to an Office they are almost harassed to preach, teach, or something. I always say it takes a special woman to be the wife of a Pastor, because I believe it. I don't know if they are "Called" to be Pastor's wives, but they are definitely destined to be (I think). It's the same for husbands called to be married to female Pastors. From what I've heard Joyce Meyer's husband is an excellent example.

Pray for them, don't judge them. Pray for them; don't spread disparaging remarks about them. Pray for them; don't try to always get in their space. Pray for them and don't place them on pedestals as if they were super humans, then have a hissy fit when they act like HUMAN BEINGS.

Another pertinent issue is congregant's mistaken perception that they need to quite frequently speak with their Pastors and their wives. Quite frankly what really needs to happen are those who believe they are called to Ministerial Offices need to talk to the Apostles, Prophets, and Teachers. Those who have questions about faith, church stuff, Body of Christ issues, gifts, and other life issues need to talk to Teachers, Evangelists, Apostles, those with the Gift to Rule, and Prophets.

This is another reason why all the Offices working together in churches is so important. I guess some Pastors like all the attention, but I feel sorry for those who are hurt, and even die spiritually (sometimes physically) because their Pastors neglect to work as a team with those God sends to help, or they refuse to train those who are called to Ministerial Offices who also have been sent to help.

One last thing, for those Pastor's spouses who are not called to a specific Office, I believe God bestows various gifts (see Epilogue) on them as needed to support, encourage, help, direct, and protect their spouses'. You may never see it. You aren't supposed to. They have the trust of their spouse and that is as it should be.

5
The Bedroom Teacher

Acts 13:1; In the church at Antioch there were prophets and teachers: Barnabas, Simeon called Niger, Lucius of Cyrene, Manaen (who had been brought up with Herod the tetrarch) and Saul. (http://bible.cc/acts/13-1.htm)

Studying the lives of these men (the ones who were teachers) will help you understand the role of teachers.

The Bedroom is a place where we feel comfortable, rest, rejuvenate, dress, undress, and love others. So it is with the Office of the Teacher. They help us feel comfortable in the Body of Christ; help us to learn who we are in Christ. Teachers teach us how to rest in Lord, how to Love our neighbors as ourselves, how to love the Lord with all our heart, mind, and strength. We learn to be comfortable with who we are in Christ, because Teachers teach us about our spiritual gifts and callings.

We are able to be ourselves and see ourselves in the mirrors, because they reveal or help us to reveal our nakedness (our strengths, faults, needs, weaknesses) and then they teach us to clothe ourselves in Christ's righteousness.

We learn we are covered by the Precious Blood of Jesus, and what that means to us, and for us. We are able to find support in the manner and amount we need it from the pillows, mattresses, and chairs. Teachers speak to the things we have tucked away privately in our drawers and closets.

The Office of Teacher builds upon the topics Pastors preach, which is why many Pastors are Teachers, also. Teachers teach the basic principles of The Word of God. They are not concerned about feeding people. However, today some people do keep snacks, microwaves and mini refrigerators in their bedrooms. These "Snacks" are usually not healthy. Sometimes they are, but Teachers have to be careful about trying to appeal to people's cravings for "goodies". The lesson is what the lesson is. The principle is the principle. Faith comes by hearing, so if we are listening our faith will grow stronger in the area in which the Teacher is teaching.

All Teachers are different. They have their own style just as we pick the style in which we decorate our bedrooms. Some are more passionate and inspire passion like a bedroom decorated in red. Some are calming like a room decorated in blue. Some are really down to earth like a room decorated in earth tones. Some teachers are really positive. They can make the most horrible situation seem like a blessing. They are like a yellow room. Yes, there can be a combination of colors such as a passionate positive Teacher.

Many Bedrooms today have attached Bathrooms exemplifying their close relationship. For instance, after you've been undressed in the Bedroom you take a shower in the Bathroom, or once you've awakened from a nice sleep you take a shower to wash off all the dead skin you shed during the night. Many people also have exercise equipment in their Bedrooms, so after they've sweated, worked on getting fit, they go to the Bathroom to clean or freshen up, Amen.

6
The Bathroom Prophet

Deuteronomy 18:18; I will raise up for them a Prophet like you from among their brethren, and will put My words in His mouth, and He shall speak to them all that I commend Him.

(/passage/?search=Deuteronomy+18:18&version=NKJV) biblegateway.com

The Book of Acts is a great place to study Prophets.

The Bathroom represents the Office of the Prophet. Remember, God told me I was Bathroom so the revelation started with this room. I must admit I wasn't happy thinking about myself as a toilet. Initially all I saw was a toilet (like the one on the cover of this book) filled with waste, spit, vomit, and dirt; the yucky stuff. However, as the Lord began to expand the vision from a toilet to an entire bathroom I began to understand how the role of the Office of the Prophet is tied to the skills of knowing whether a situation calls for the tub, shower, toilet, sink, medicine cabinet, etc.

The Bathroom is the place where we go to relieve ourselves, clean ourselves, relax, groom ourselves, tend to our wounds, and fix our flaws. We can see ourselves in the mirror, which is revelation. People can come to us with their crap, with the stuff that needs to be regurgitated. We flush it and they feel better. Some people have chaise lounges and coffee in their bathrooms. They relax in there and read. Some read to be informed, others to laugh. Prophets can inform and be a source of exuberant relief, also.

Looking into the medicine cabinet is also revealing to the purpose of the Prophet. Some people need a Band-Aid to cover a wound. Others only need some ointment to protect them from infection. Some people need to cover flaws on their face, in their mouth, on their heads, etc. These various covering represent our prayers.

We brush our teeth with toothpaste. The toothpaste represents the words we speak in accordance with God's Word and direction.

At other times someone who is constipated might need some laxatives. Those operating in the Office of the Prophet can discern when a person is stuck due to an issue or they're holding on to something and are finding it difficult to let go of it (like something that hurt them in their past). Prophets can pray in such a way that the person is able to release it.

I am going to write this: those called to the Office the Prophet address the stuff that both other Ministers don't want to address and stuff other ministers shouldn't have to address. I'm telling you some of the smells and goings on in the Bathroom is strictly for the Bathroom. That's why air freshener is so wonderful, Praise God! Those operating in the Office of the Prophet are able to usher in the sweet aroma of the Holy Spirit. We learn from the Bible that love covers a multitude of sins (1Peter 4:8). In that sweet anointed aroma sin can't thrive. Especially, in the corporate anointing Prophet's anointing can usher in such a presence of the Lord that the miraculous can occur. If you've ever been in service where the anointing was very thick I can guarantee that a Prophet was there.

What else is unique about this Ministry? Someone with a gastrointestinal issue could be a problem. Someone with a gastrointestinal issue represents a person who consistently faces issues because they talk too much, or they are verbally abusive and hurt people's feelings, or they are mean. If this person consistently seeks the ministry of a Prophet for guidance the problems manifest because instead of relying on God and the Holy Spirit they try to rely on the Prophet. This is important because the Office of the Prophet is not fortune telling. It is foretelling as God Wills. They can't just access the anointing because someone wants them to. They proclaim what God is going to do as the Lord wills. That is how you know if they are true Prophets, if what they say comes to pass. Here again, the Pastor, Teacher, and Prophet are needed to inform and educate this person about the correct role of the Prophet, prophecy, as well as, life, communication, interpersonal, and emotional management skills. People need to understand that 1.) Prophets don't guide and 2.) The Lord directs people through their inner witness, and unction (a knowing given by the Holy Spirit) and His Word.

Prophets can run off at the mouth, also. A Prophet who always wants to tell you about yourself and tell you what to do is like a person with diarrhea. Yes, there are false prophets. This is why many people (some Pastors) are hesitant to allow and acknowledge the Prophetic Gift. However, God knew this so He instituted the process and procedure of Prophets being subject to other Prophets, because false prophets can wreak havoc in churches. That's right. You've heard the term "game recognizes game"? Well, Prophets recognize Prophetic utterances. Praise God! That is why all of the Gifts need to be educated, trained, mentored, and allowed to operate in church. It may be that instead of being a false prophet the person is just an untrained, uneducated Prophet who was not mentored.

Let me explain what I mean about Prophets recognizing/confirming/evaluating other Prophets words. I can be talking with one my friends in Cleveland about a subject (based on the Word of God) when He'll illuminate a particular point. I can receive a call from a friend in California who tells me she and a friend were discussing the very same thing. Then I can call a friend in Texas who informs me that he was praying and the Lord revealed the same thing to him. God confirms His Word with two or three witnesses always based on His Word. If this can happen across the continent isn't it reasonable that it this can occur in a church, also?

Churches need to have set procedures Prophets can follow when they have a word for the Body of Christ. Do they walk up to the front, inform a certain member of the staff, just speak out during Praise and Worship, or raise their hand? What I use to do at one church when the Lord gave me a word was write the Pastors a note. They would read it and give me permission to speak.

At another church I would write the actual prophecy and give it to the Pastor only. That was cool for him, but not for the church because they were not edified. He might mention the topic over the pulpit, though. I believe God watches over His Word to perform it regardless of who speaks it. The only thing is that I know the anointing on a Prophetic word spoken by a Prophet is different; it's stronger.

At another church I was hesitant to speak because I didn't know the procedure. After church when I told my Pastor I hadn't given the word the Lord gave me, he admonished me to never do that again. He told me if I had a word to just give it. However, because I didn't want to be out of order, since something was always going on during the service, it was very difficult for me to flow in my gift. If he had said, "O.K., if you get a word during Praise and Worship give it either at the end of a song, or give it before we pray, or before I preach, or give it at the end of church before the benediction" I would have been more confident. However, I it really is more about flowing with the Holy Spirit than it is about confidence.

That's another thing the prophecy of true prophets edifies the Body of Christ. All that "you are cursed stuff" and "God is going to get you" is a direct result of ignorance and/or self-condemnation. These are not messages God gives His Prophets. Proclamations like this are indicative of a constipated Prophet. These messages are evidence that the anointing is not flowing. Please don't misunderstand me, God can and does use prophecy to correct, but it's not abusive. You may feel like you've been shaken, but that is just you (your spirit) recognizing that God has your number and is really concerned about every detail of your life.

Prophets can give "If you" "Then I" prophecies like if you keep your mind focused on me I will keep you in peace that passes all understanding, or If you put me first I will give you the desires of your heart". However, Prophets don't say things like "If you sin I will kill you" "If you disobey me I will take what you have and your latter state will be worse than your beginning". We can say things like, "I've seen your tears and heard your cries, I am God I change not, I Love you my child. Don't give up; don't lose faith. Focus on the issues of your life. Seek my face, seek my face. Your work and labor for me is not in vain, thus saith the Lord".

I remember one time the Lord told me to talk to a lady suffering from drug addiction. The first time I talked to her (privately) I told her the Lord wanted to heal her, but she had to seriously seek assistance to gain control of the addiction. I told her that if she continued to use drugs she could die. This was not some super spiritual proclamation. It was just a fact, drugs can kill. Addictions can kill and not just chemical addictions. Workaholics can work themselves to death; food addicts can eat themselves to death; gamblers can get into situations where someone kills them because they either owe money or have won a lot of money. So those addicted to chemicals should not be treated and looked upon as if they have three heads or something. They are ill just like sex addicts or any other addict. Anyway, the second time (during a church service) the Lord had me talk to this lady He actually gave me a "Word" for her. In that "Word" I mentioned nothing about death, but the Lord told her He would heal her. I was told that she went to an addiction center far from her home. I was told she is ordained, preaching, and is drug free, Praise God!

Then there is the area of the pipes in the Bathroom. I love this. When the Lord revealed this to me I was so excited. In the natural I would not want anything to do with this, but I realized without it the actual Bathroom would be worthless and useless. He said the media and a lot of people like to depict black and dark

God Did You Call Me A Toilet?

things with negative connotations, but there are useful, necessary, and good things that go on in the dark and that are black. He said when a seed is planted in the ground it is dark in the ground, but life is growing; growth is taking place in the darkness. He continued with, "A baby in the womb grows in the dark. He said the pipes in the walls of a bathroom are in the dark". He told me the water necessary for the shower; the tub; the sink, and toilet are made available by way of the pipes. Similarly, the only way the soiled water leaves the Bathroom is by way of the pipes. My anointing flows through you the same way. As pipes in the bathroom get backed up and clogged you must ensure you keep your heart clean and pure before me. You must forgive people as I forgive you. You must love people as I love you".

    The tub and shower are amazing, too. People can take rejuvenating, refreshing, or exhilarating showers, and calming, or therapeutic baths. The bathroom can be a really nice space in which to luxuriate. However, it can be a dangerous place, especially the tub. If people are not careful they can slip, fall, crack their heads, and even drown. The implications for Prophets here are astounding. Trying to make a prophecy or telling a lie as you prophesy can have devastating consequences to those to whom the Prophets is speaking with and the Prophet, as well. Playing around with people verbally when you occupy this Office is risky, because I've seen situations where what is said comes to pass. So Prophets have to be careful and watch what they say all time.

    Prophets also offer support to keep people from slipping and falling just as the non-slip decals on the bottom of the tub and the rails inside the tub. Those tools and skills help people maintain their balance, get up (not just from falls), and get down safely (find strength as they traverse life's situations). The support the Office of the Prophet provides is different from the support one receives in the Living Room, Dining Room, Kitchen or Bedroom. In the first 3 you usually don't sit or walk around in them wet and naked. While you can walk around the Bedroom wet and naked you usually don't lie in bed that way, unless you are wet from sweating.

Those called to the Office of the Prophet are adept at providing the tools necessary for "people" to cleanse themselves (soap, wash cloths, sponges, and towels). Adding aroma therapy and light therapy takes the experience to another level. In the case of Christians this process is just informing and reminding them that Jesus is their righteousness; that Jesus covered and paid for their sin. This removes guilt and self-condemnation which is a source of self-injury for some, because the Holy Spirit convicts us. He doesn't condemn us. We do that to ourselves and others.

The Holy Spirit can really manifest His Power through Prophets when the Minister of Music and the Choir are in the Spirit. It is like they are the water heater. (I just got this and every house needs a water heater, Praise God!). Oh, Praise God I just got this, too. The sink in the Bathroom holds water, just like the sink in the Kitchen. They both hold water which is related to their anointing, but their anointing is for different administrations of the Spirit or for different purposes.

Another profoundly genuine aspect of the Bathroom is the ability to hold water in the tub. This represents the need to both store large amounts of water (anointing) and to access large amounts of water (anointing). The level or volume of water in the tub is directly determined by the music. Music that speaks to the Prophet's spirit will increase the volume or level of the anointing, regardless of where they are. Lord, have mercy. Why? It's tied to purpose. Storing large of amounts of anointing allows the Prophet to cover, even submerge people in the anointing. There's something important about storing large amounts of water; Prophets can't hold that water for a long time. The purpose is related to the temperature of the water.

Storing large amounts of hot water (not scalding, comfortable) because of the water heater (Oh my) signifies that God is about to do something corporately. It can happen wherever the Prophet is when anointed music is playing that speaks to their spirit. Storing large amounts of tepid water (like when a baby has a high fever and needs to be immersed in the water to bring down her temperature) is for specific situations that don't happen often, such as emergencies or something therapeutic.

Cold water can remain in the tub longer, but rarely is it. For example, on a really hot day in a home with no air conditioner someone might put on their trunks (or not) and sit in the tub to cool off. My husband and I have done this in the shower, but I'll get to the shower in a minute. With most homes having modern conveniences not many people see the need to sit in cold water. It's not necessary, but I understand athletes sit in ice tubs for their muscles. Similarly, to the poor and those that are suffering or tortured believe me that cold water is a welcome relief when things "heat up" in one's life, as it were.

Accessing large amounts of water is important when it is time to pray (like when something is being birthed in the spirit), or when it is time to lay hands on someone, or to join someone in faith, or believe for a miracle. This type of ministering takes a while. Remember, when Elisha laid on the person to bring them back to life. He covered him with his body, with the anointing in his body. It's like that, because it takes time to fill the tub up with water.

I told you I'd get to the shower. Some Kitchens and Bathrooms have the ability to spray water. Remember, not all Kitchens have that retractable hose, but those that do usually have the ability to spray the vegetables or fruit. So if the Pastor sprays, she is spraying specifically in the sink for a specific reason that is related to food, meat or fruit, unless the purpose is to clean the actual sink. Food and meat reference the Word of God. Fruit refers to the Fruit of the Spirit. Pastors can spray them to clean them, make them grow or make them stand out. If a person takes that hose and sprays all over the Kitchen someone is going to have a mess to clean up.

It is almost the same for the shower, except the Prophet has the ability to cover or spray a larger area. I've experienced this before in church corporate settings when the anointing was high during Praise and Worship. I could sense the anointing cover me and spread throughout the congregation. You can't take a shower in the kitchen sink. In the shower your entire body is covered with water. In the newer more expensive homes the homeowners have the option of installing targeted massaging showerheads. I've experienced this, too. I concentrated my prayer on the Pastor while he was preaching, or praying, or on someone the Lord pointed out in the Spirit. For instance, the Lord may say there is someone else here who is thinking about getting saved or who is hurting. I would pray (really pray) while that anointing was operating through me, then another person would accept the Lord, or go up for prayer, or stand up and give a testimony depending on which church I was attending at the time.

The Prophet has to know when hot water is needed, when cold water is needed, and when tepid water is needed. They can sense when the stream of water needs to be hard, fast, slow, or light. If the Prophet is not careful someone can be scaled. If you are frostbitten and you put your hands in hot water your hands can be permanently damaged. Prophets have to be careful to always operate in the Spirit as the Lord leads. That's what often deters them from being obedient and from other leaders trusting them. However, it is necessary for the other 5-Fold Ministers to understand the Prophet's role, because after someone had come out of something, when they are spent the heat lamp feels wonderful. It warms them when they are cold and dries them when they are wet.

The mirror in the bathroom is cool like the mirrors in the bedroom. It is important for Prophets to self-reflect also. Self-care is really important, just as it is for the other 5-Fold Ministers. These Ministries are really draining on the minister as the flow of water illustrates. Revelation knowledge about the Body of Christ, about how best to instruct people (not guide them) is corroborated by the mirrors presence in the Bathroom. People are naked to prophets because they can "see" the real person; the spirit of the person. They don't have to hide, because when the anointing is operating they can't, anyway. Read 1 Corinthians 14:14-16 which is talking about the Gift of Divers Kinds of Tongues needing Interpretation to be effective. Well, Tongues and Interpretation are equivalent to Prophecy. The Bible says the secrets of the person's heart are revealed by this ministry. Prophets often operate in the Gifts of Divers Kinds of Tongues and Interpretation, too.

Reflecting on the role and responsibility of the Office of Prophet illuminated the need for the bathroom to always pray and not to faint. Also, Prophets must remember that Jesus is their righteousness. You all know men spray and kids miss the bowl sometimes, so bathrooms get dirty. People who keep rugs in front of the toilet surely have urine sprinkles on them which are tracked into other parts of the house. What about the splash from vomit, sometimes it gets on the walls.

Cleaning the actual toilet is of course a must. I can't even begin to address the amount of attention that is needed to manage the spirits of people who are full of speech having idiotic tendencies that needs to be flushed down the toilet. But the toilet holds water, too. The water (anointing) functions to (1) keep the bowl clean when waste is deposited into it (2) make the depositing of waste into the bowl easier, you know the plop, plop, plop, and (3) make the flushing of waste easier. A friend told me about a dream she's had in which a toilet had a leak. What does a leak in the toilet mean? There is a problem with the prophet's anointing to dispose of waste. They need to seek the Lord or assistance from another 5-Fold Minister to find out why they are holding on to either other people's or their own crap.

The residue from dirt in the sink or tub has to be cleaned. Prophets can't keep people's stuff. They can't allow other people's issues to get tracked into their lives or their spirits. So they have to be avid prayers. They are skilled at knowing what gets flushed and what goes down the sink, tub, or shower drains.

God Did You Call Me A Toilet?

I realized something else about bathrooms. There are 2 types of people who go to the bathroom, those who are happy, who like going to the bathroom. These people spend a lot of time in there. You know the ones their family members are constantly complaining about, because they won't come out of the bathroom.

Then there are those who don't like going to the bathroom. They hold their urine until the last minute and rush out immediately after relieving themselves. I've seen people in such a hurry to get out of the Bathroom that they don't wash their hands, which means they've either missed what the Prophet was saying, or they've misinterpreted the message. In the latter case they can spread those germs, as it were, to others. It doesn't matter which type of person one is, because everyone, eventually, has to go to the bathroom.

It is the same with people's perception of Prophets. Some people like them and actually go to them because they respect them. Others don't really value them, don't want to hear them, and basically don't believe in this gift. It doesn't matter though, because the words spoken by true Prophets will bless those to whom their words are spoken and will come true whether folks heed them or not. The last thing people should know about Prophets is they **DON'T KNOW EVERYTHING**.

If you are "Called" to the Office of Prophet spend some time looking at all the things in your bathroom to see if you can discern how they can be useful in ministry.

7
Combined Rooms

Jesus is the best example of someone holding and/or operating in multiple offices. He is a teacher, evangelist and prophet. Some people even called him the Head Apostle. Studying his life should prove enjoyable.

There are times when people have multiple gifts like the Prophetic Teacher which is the Bedroom/Bathroom combo. This person teaches, but there's a strong revelatory anointing on their teaching. People are healed, people cry during their messages. It's amazing. There's the Evangelistic Pastor which is the Living Room/Kitchen combo in which people are saved in large numbers. This Pastor probably travels quite a bit. There is the Apostolic Pastor who has what we call Sister Churches birthed out of their original ministry. They travel to other ministries to mentor other Pastors and train them.

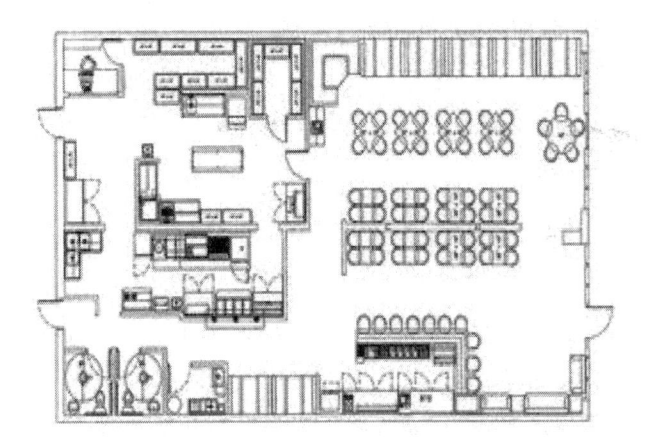

Inside of restaurant depicting joint ministries. Bathroom stalls (bottom left), Kitchen (middle and upper left), Dining area (middle right).

Consider for example the rare occasions when some ministers are extremely anointed and hold 3 Offices. A minister holding and Evangelistic, Apostolic, Pastor Office travels, people are saved wherever they go, they mentor others, and yet pastor their own church. Consider the Prophetic, Teaching, Pastor who has a strong anointing, is an excellent teacher who pastors a church. This Pastor travels quite a bit, as well.

Restaurants and fast food establishments are great illustrations of these combinations (refer to illustration above). In a restaurant like a McDonalds there is a kitchen, bathroom, and a dining area. There are other combinations based on what the Body of Christ needs.

In our churches all of the Offices should operate together as they do in the Body of Christ. There are times when particular Offices or 5-Fold Ministers will work together specifically such as major spiritual events like convocations, retreats, advances, and other special church events. The purpose of the event will dictate which offices and gifts are needed.

8
Epilogue

I Corinthians 7:7b; But every man hath his proper gift of God, one after this manner, and another after that.

(The Open Bible NKJV, Thomas Nelson Publishers, Nashville, TN © Copyright, 1983, 1985, 1990, 1997).

Everyone is not called to a 5-Fold Ministry. Everyone has a gift, though.

Not everyone is called to a 5-Fold Ministry. Everyone has a gift, though. I Corinthians 7:7b; But every man hath his proper gift of God, one after this manner, and another after that.

In Romans 12:6-8 we read, Having then gifts differing according to the grace that is given to us, whether prophecy, let us prophesy according to the proportion of faith; or ministry, let us wait on our ministering: or he that teacheth, on teaching; or he that exhoreth, on exhortation: he that giveth, let him do it with simplicity; he that ruleth, with diligence; he that showeth mercy, with cheerfulness. But wait, there's more! I Corinthians 12:4-11 informs us that "NOW" there are diversities of gifts, but the same Spirit, and there are differences of administration, but the same Lord, and there are diversities of operations, but it is the same God which worketh all in all, but the manifestation of the Spirit is given to every man to profit withal. For to one is given by the Spirit the <u>word of wisdom</u>; to another the <u>word of knowledge</u> by the same Spirit; to another <u>faith</u> by the same Spirit; to another the <u>gifts of healing</u> by the same Spirit; to another the <u>working of miracles</u>; to another prophecy; to another <u>discerning of spirits</u>; to another <u>divers kinds of tongues</u>; but all these worketh that one and the selfsame Spirit, dividing to every man severally as He will.

First, we will open up these scriptures. You can explore the biblical instructions regarding how we should conduct ourselves in ministry found in Romans 12:9-21, and Chapters 13, 14, and 15:1-14.

For my Biblical scholars and those who question or doubt this revelation the Lord gave me, who would point out the fact that there are Deacons, Minsters of Music and Song, Dancers, Bishops, etc. in the Body of Christ. I say you are absolutely right. These are other gifts in the Body of Christ, as well. If you are called to one of these work them in love, with all of your might. Others will say there are other rooms in some houses. What about the Den, Exercise Room, Patio, Basement, etc. Heck, one lady had a Bird Room and a Gift Wrap Room. Some people have Wine Cellars and rooms as Humidors. These are other gifts in the Body of Christ, as well. If you are called to one of these ministries work in it. These people are absolutely correct, but this is not the book that explores all the gifts God bestows. He only gave me the revelation for the 5-Fold Ministry. Therefore, I am just going to stay in my lane. Feel free to write that book if God gives you that revelation. I'd love to read it, Amen.

Now back to the above scriptures. This book is not about all the other gifts in the Body of Christ, so I will not delve into them, in detail. All of the Gifts God bestows on and in the Body of Christ are Graces. They are Grace Gifts. We didn't earn them. We did nothing to deserve to "BE" them or receive them. However, we should be gracious enough to receive the "people" with the gifts (who are the Gifts, literally) when God sends them to us.

Aside from those called to the Office of Prophet, there are those who have the <u>Gift of Prophecy</u>. This means according to their faith they prophesy when needed in the Body. It's the same with those who have the <u>Gift of Teaching</u> when needed, but are not called to Office of Teacher. These people are to wait on their ministry. What do they do while waiting. Study, learn, or spend time with Prophets and Teachers. They should learn about their gifts; learn how to operate in their gifts. It is the same with <u>Exhorters</u>, people who inspire other. They are to wait on their ministry, as well. All of the 5-Fold Ministers can train and mentor them.

I'm going to say it. There needs to be more mentoring and training in the Body of Christ. Not just workshops or seminars held once a year, but on-going training and mentoring because people are being saved every day. People are discovering their calling every day. People have questions about their purpose every day.

Alright, back to the scriptures. Some are called with the <u>Gift of Giving;</u> they are to give simply, not with elaborate pomp and circumstance every time God tells them to give something. Some give money, some give stuff, some give time. The simplicity part is really important, so those called to this ministry need to study how to give, because giving so everybody knows many bring the immediate praise of people, but blurs the actual giving and gift from spiritual standpoint. It's a matter of motive.

Some are called with the <u>Gift to Rule</u>. I think Apostles operate in this Gift. They are to do so diligently, not abusively, not hard-nosed, not arrogantly. Look up the word diligent. Take it apart and put it back together with the word rule. I talk about "ruling" within a home in my book, **ANOINTED** Married Christian Men, because we are so often told that men rule the home and their wives; often the meaning is grossly improperly presented. So study to show yourself approved unto God, it will avoid shame, later.

Some people have the <u>Gift of Showing Mercy</u>. This is an awesome gift. They are supposed to do so cheerfully. So if you are not a cheerful person you probably don't have this gift.

Some people may be called to the same gift as someone else, but the way in which it is administered or operates may differ. That is fine. That's what the Word says and how the Lord Wills it, Amen. We shouldn't try to "be like" that person. We are not carbon copies of other people. We should try to look like Jesus, period, in whatever our Gifting. I've seen this go both ways.

Pastors usually are more vulnerable to this area because they seek out people they can mold into "clones". They are usually the ones appointing positions in the church, or they are drawn to people in whom they see themselves. It is natural to be drawn to someone with the attributes we admire in ourselves. The problem arises when Pastors overlook, ignore, or reject those really called to ministry because they are not like them.

However, the Office of Pastor is a supernatural call (as are all the 5-Fold Ministers). God should be the one leading the Pastors to their mentees. I'm not picking on the Pastors. It happens more with them just because they are more exposed; people have more access to them. Some people esteem them more highly than they should so Pastors often become targets of the enemy. Can you see where problems can arise?

What if all the Kitchens were yellow, where would the green, white, or country Kitchen be? I guess some would say at another church. I hear that, but the warning is to be careful to listen to God as you choose whom to train, with whom to minister, and as you discern whom is "Called" to Ministry and who is not. Remember, the story of David. David's Dad just knew one of his other bigger, older sons was the one the Prophet wanted who would be King, but no, he wanted the smallest, dirtiest, smelliest son. Caution is warranted, Amen.

I love God. He knew some people would be leery of the Gifts; of having them operate so all may profit (holistically) together. The Late Rev. Kenneth E. Hagin wrote some books entitled; *Understanding the Anointing* (1996, 1983 RHEMA Bible Church), and *He Gave Gifts unto Men* (1992, RHEMA Bible Church) which really explain the gifts and offices. I'm not sure if they are still in print, but I think they are excellent resources. He discusses our individual anointing and our corporate anointing. Also, Dr. Bill Hamon has a book entitled, The Day of The Saints (2002, Destiny Image © Publishers, Inc.) which is another excellent resource on this topic.

The Gift of <u>Word of Wisdom</u> is a foretelling of future events. Again, it must be stated that it is not fortune telling. People should not be walking up to folks always trying to tell them what God has to say to them. That is not a Word of Wisdom.

Those who operate in the Gift of the <u>Word of Knowledge</u> reveal facts known by God.

The Bible informs us that we all have a measure of faith and that Jesus was given faith without measure. Well, those with the Gift of Faith are bestowed the ability to believe supernaturally. I mean this is special Faith. Let me see if I can help you understand this. Say there was someone in the congregation with a congenital disease, disorder, or someone was injured beyond repair in an accident. The doctors have said there is nothing we can do for these people. They will spend their lives this way. Next, let's say the person with the Gifts of Healing senses that God is leading them to pray for these people (the pastor and all those "Called" would be notified and the pastor would have to say go ahead).

Alright, as the person with the Gifts of Healing is praying the person with the Gift of Faith would join with that person (with the Gifts of Healing) and her anointing would join with, support, make stronger the prayer to reverse the congenital disease or disorder, and the limbs or whatever had been damaged in the accident.

People with the <u>Gift of Faith</u> can believe for anything, jobs, bills, finances, favor, etc. I know a Pastor with this Gift. He came to my house one evening. Everyone he prayed for that night was blessed. One lady got a new car, 2 people received jobs, another lady was going to be homeless and jobless and both needs were met. He has an amazing Gift of Faith.

God bestows the <u>Gifts of Healing</u> on people as He wills. They don't walk in, as it were, all the time. They sense the anointing to heal all over their body. Notice that it is Gift"**S**" of Healing. Some people's anointing may only heal certain things like cancers, or the internal wounds of abuse, or coma's. This is why all those with this Gift should be mentored and encouraged. We need them. This is also why all the Gifts of the Holy Spirit should be allowed to operate. Do you agree?

In the above mentioned scenario I can see how someone with Gift of the Working of Miracles would be important, too. Can't you? People have told stories of miracles happening in their lives. Yes, sometimes it's the work of angels, but maybe sometimes it's the prayer of those with Gift of the Working of Miracles that causes the miraculous to manifest. I believe this Gift should manifest in church, in the street, in our homes, in jail, and in the hospitals. Once all the gifts are allowed to manifest and operate we will see the "greater works" mentioned in the Bible.

God chooses to anoint people to <u>Prophesy</u> whenever he needs them to. These people don't have to hold the Office of the Prophet to operate in the Gift of Prophecy. Some may only do it once. Others may do it occasionally, as the Lord Wills. Jesus and Paul did this.

People operating in the <u>Gift of Discerning of Spirits</u> can recognize what spirit is operating, motivating a person. It's as if they can see it.

The <u>Gift of Divers Kinds of Tongues</u> is coupled with the <u>Gift of Interpretations of Tongues</u> discussed in I Corinthians 14:28. When they are combined they equal prophecy. This is interesting because a person can actually speak in Divers Kinds of Tongues and interpret them. Conversely, one person can speak in Divers Kinds of Tongues while someone else interprets the message. This can happen with songs, also. Another important point is that the message is interpreted, not translated. So the actual length of the Divers Kinds of Tongues may not equal the length of the Interpretation.

I have to tell you a story about the Gift of Divers Kinds of Tongues and Interpretation. One morning the women of our church attended a women's breakfast at another church. As we were in praise and worship someone operated in the Gift of Divers Kinds of Tongues. The Holy Spirit told me who had the Interpretation. So we all waited, and waited, and waited. As we waited we prayed. I kept praying for the woman with the Interpretation to speak, but she didn't. Finally, the Holy Spirit gave me the Interpretation so I spoke it forth. After praise and worship ended I went over to the woman who initially had the Interpretation. I told her the Holy Spirit told me she had it. She said, "I know, I know. I prayed and asked Him to give it to you."

The moral of the story is God will not make you speak. The Holy Spirit will give you the unction, but you have to open your mouth to speak. He doesn't give you the entire message all at once, either. He gives you the beginning of it. Then as you begin to speak the rest flows, and it is always in line with the Word of God. The message is not a doom and gloom, hell fire and damnation message. It is an encouraging, empowering, assuring message.

This is why all the members of the church need to be aware of false messages and false prophets as I said earlier. They also need to recognize when someone is operating in any of the vocal gifts without the leading of the Holy Spirit. Again this is why the Prophets are subject to the Prophets.

In I Corinthians 1 Paul is talking to the church established at Corinth. In verse 7a he says, "So that you come behind in no gift." I said in the preceding chapters that neither we nor others can stop God from doing what He Wills in our lives concerning the use of our Calls or Gifts. I know God can lead us to other places and people to accomplish His Will if the initial person or place becomes or serves as a hindrance. This scripture confirms that we can "come behind" be late, be hindered; or not be as fully active when we should.

The Apostle in 1 Corinthians 1:7; came to ensure they (all the members of the church at Corinth) did not come behind in their spiritual gifts. This includes those holding 5-Fold Ministry Offices. Why is this important? One woman went to her Pastor to tell him she was leaving his church because she was called to the Office of Prophetess (a female Prophet) and was not able to flow in her gifts at that church. Her Pastor told her he knew she was called to that ministry and he knew she had to leave because she needed more. He said he wasn't the one to give it to her and his church was not that kind of church or something that alluded to that.

This is such a lie of Satan, such a distortion of fact. He was saying I'm a Kitchen, but I can't feed you. Look my specialty is bologna and I refuse to make you a corned beef sandwich. You say you need corned beef to live; well you have to go get it somewhere else. Wow! Remember, it's the Kitchens job to ensure there is both enough food for everyone, and that the Kitchen had enough tools (Gifts) to carry out the tasks needed in the Body of Christ at their particular churches.

Another Prophetess approached her Pastor to give him a prophecy God had given her for him. He rejected it. He told her if God had a word for him, He'd give it to him directly, because he knew God. She was devastated, because she was walking in love, obeying what God told her to do. She actually believed her Pastor trusted her since she was licensed and ordained by him. She didn't understand the rejection since he allowed her preach in his church. She was so hurt she left that church.

There are probably thousands of stories like this. All those rejected, hurt, devastated saints of God and Ministers in and to the Body of Christ need healing ministered to them. How sad that the hurt came from someone who was charged with their care and growth. Well, in the real world I guess the shepherd does harm his sheep...when he kills them. The difference is the shepherd harms his sheep to feed and clothe others, while Pastors who harm their sheep forget Jesus is all of our sacrificial lamb, who left the Holy Spirit here, who chooses to work His Gifts through us to bless The Body of Christ that includes Pastors.

A Pastor can and should reject the Word a Prophet has if it is not edifying or if it is not based on or in line with the Word of God. A word can also be rejected if it is just outrageous. For instance, pretend you think Jaguars are hideous and can't stand them. Then I tell you not to buy a Jaguar, because if you do you'll drive off a cliff. Now that is definitely a word to reject. Maybe, that's what happened with them (her prophecy was ridiculous). I don't know.

It is possible the word she had was a Word of Wisdom regarding something that is going to "be". However, if a Prophet's prophecy is just outrageous it is the Pastor's responsibility to ensure that other Offices are in operation at that church so the Prophet receives Prophetic Mentoring. If the word just doesn't agree with the Pastor's spirit the Pastor can do as my Southern California Pastor used to do, sit it on a shelf until later. There were also times when either a member of the church or someone visiting with a demonic spirit spoke a word that was not in line with the Word of God. Pastor would let them finish. Then he would say we don't receive that word because it is not in line with the Word of God. He would then read the scriptures regarding the elements of true prophecies. However, if the person was really outrageous the Pastor would have the Deacons escort them outside, but he would still read the scriptures to avoid confusion.

If the word was delivered by a person with a demonic spirit he would also read the scriptures regarding everything being done decently and in order, because they had spoken out of turn, interrupted the service without permission, and they were not 5-Fold Ministers at that church. He did all this to ensure all the members of his congregation (baby, teen, and mature Christians) were informed and educated about true Prophets and true prophecy. This consistent reiteration built faith for prophecy and confidence in the various forms of prophecy.

Do you know why the other Pastor was not able to help, understand, or receive the ministry of these Prophetesses'? It's because he would not acknowledge the Offices of Apostle, Prophet, and Teacher in his church. They would have helped him grow, they would have grown, and together the congregation would have grown. They could have shown him where to purchase the best corned beef, how to cook it properly, and finally how to serve it properly. They would have imparted gifts to him which he needed to help the members of his congregation grow in their spiritual gifts while utilizing their own gifts to help him grow, as well. Finally, they are able to evaluate each other as they minister to offer corrective performance improvement suggestions. This is so important. Choosing to neglect, to fully utilize all the Gifts of God is negatively impacting local churches, local communities, the Body of Christ, and the World.

The Bible tells us that we (Christians) are supposed to do greater works than Jesus. Jesus raised people from the dead. I asked God about this one day. I asked Him what is greater than raising people from the dead. You know what He said. He said, "Stop them from dying." That's right if we were doing our collective, COLLECTIVE jobs our kids would not be dying in the streets by the thousands all over the World. Men would not be killing themselves and their families. Our teenagers would not be committing suicide. Our youth would not be leaving The Church. People would not be foregoing marriage for other options. Hate groups should not be growing. People should not be disrespecting our President.

I don't know what "The Church" is doing. Some churches have made some progress in some areas. I know there are a great number of churches doing amazing things in their communities. I know some churches are doing as much as they can. I am not talking about churches doing things that take finances or donations. I'm talking about "spirit issues" "issues of the heart", Holy Spirit Powered issues", not human powered feats. I praise God for all "The Church" is doing to bless people.

However, we should not be the largest hate group in the World based on fear, ignorance, and/or pride. Yes, I said it. The Church "our churches" are so full of "isms" it is a shame. If you aren't familiar with these "isms" let me show you what they sound like.

Sexism – Women should be quiet. They aren't leading men in this church. Shoot, they are too emotional.

Ageism – We need young blood, or the opposite, that child is too young to do anything.

Elitism - Oh, they are unlearned or poor. We are the top, the best and the brightest.

Cronyism – Yes, this is my guy, yeah, he can lead this or that. Oh, he's my old frat buddy.

I don't use the word Racism because there is only one Race of people on the planet, so Racism means I hate people. I use Ethnicism – Sit "those" people in front so everyone can see we are multicultural, or, Oh, My, we can't have "those" people as members of our church they are cursed!

How about Internalized Ethnicism where one group internalizes the hate and stereotypes of the group that actually oppressed them. For instance, "Why don't they perm their hair, shave, and speak the Kings English? Pastor, you can't let them embarrass us here, in our church.

I'm trying to remember how many people Jesus and the early disciples shunned in the Upper Room. I'm trying to remember how many people were shunned by Jesus and the Apostles all those times the throngs of people followed Jesus, so much so, that they backed him up to the sea. Wait, what did Jesus do? He fed them literally and spiritually. I'm trying to remember how the

Apostles had "VIP" seating at those events. Wait, what did the Apostles do? They actually served the people. I'm trying to remember the address to Jesus' Church. Oh, in the streets, in the parks, in the homes of believer's and non-believers.

I'm not saying 5-Fold Ministers should serve people food. I know in Acts 6 the Apostles told **the disciples to choose leaders from among them to serve tables** so they could devote themselves to prayer **and the ministration of the word.** Wait, what was that? Doesn't Ephesians 4:12 say the **5-Fold Ministers are supposed** to see to **the complete adjustment of the saints for the work of ministration to build up the Body of Christ.**

The point is the 5-Fold Ministers were in the midst of the people. After they stopped serving tables they focused on serving up spiritual meals. Acts and Ephesians agree. Saints won't be completely adjusted (trained and mentored) inside church walls.

I will offer another word of caution here? Everyone who is Not in church is not lost or backslidden. There are a lot of Christian believers in the streets, in the highways, and hedges who are 1) seeking a church home, 2) injured or ill as a result of church folk (spiritually and emotionally), 3) ill (physically), or 4) dismayed, disgusted, disappointed, disenchanted with what goes on in churches, or 5) working in their area of ministry as the Lord has directed. I say this because they deserve respect not disdain. You'll find a surprising number of people with 5-Fold Ministry calls in those places who have active healthy relationships with other believers. Hence, they are not neglecting to come together with other saints just because they don't a particular church.

The majority of our ministering should not be taking place inside "the churches" anyway. Our kids and others are dying outside. Lord, You, know I don't want to write this, but I have to be obedient. This is a Body of Christ ISSUE! With a church on every corner and three or more in a block where is the Power of the Holy Spirit? Where are the Gifts of the Spirit? Where are the 5-Fold Ministers? I'm looking for the greater works spoken about in the Bible! I will not continue to allow the liquor stores on every corner to be more effective than "the churches"! In Jesus' Name, it is not acceptable! Where is the LOVE? Jealousy, fear, ignorance, nor pride are reasons to disobey God, let people die, let families be destroyed, or ruined when God in His infinite wisdom has provided everything we need for life and Godliness.

Come forth Apostles, Prophets (true Prophets), Pastors (after God's own heart), Evangelists, and Teachers. Come forth in Jesus' Name. Heavenly Father, I pray all the Gifts of the Holy Spirit are stirred up in the Name of Jesus in every church in Cleveland; in every church in American; in every church in the World; in every building where your called ones are located in the Name of Jesus. Heavenly Father, I thank you that we will do the greater works in Jesus' Mighty Name, according to Your Holy Will. I thank You for loving us enough to send us Gifts. Help the Pastors to receive them, in the Name of Jesus, when they walk into Your churches, Lord.

◇ ◇ ◇ ◇ ◇ ◇ ◇

Lastly, the Lord told me not to assume everyone knows that you have to be saved or born-again and filled with the Holy Spirit for any of His Gifts to operate. How do you get saved? How is one born-again? How is one filled with the Holy Spirit? You ask that's all. It's simple. You say:

> Dear God, I accept Your Son as my personal savior. I believe Jesus died on the cross for my sin and I believe He rose on the third day. Jesus I accept You as my Savior. Please come into my heart and live inside me, in Jesus' Name I thank You for saving me. Heavenly Father; thank You for the Holy Spirit being my guide, intercessor, stand-by, and helper. Holy Spirit I need You, please come into life to be my comforter with the evidence of speaking in tongues in Jesus' Name, Amen.

If you said that prayer tell someone you are saved. All heaven is rejoicing just for you right now, **Praise God!** You can speak in tongues to edify yourself whenever you get ready. Just be quiet, listen for a word or sound you've never heard before. Your first instinct will be to reject the word or sound because you'll think it sounds dumb or stupid. That is the Gift, really. Just open your mouth and say it/them. As you say it/them your spiritual vocabulary will grow. Although, some people's heavenly language just flows from the beginning. Amen.

Lord, may something You've led me to write on these pages bless someone in Jesus' Name. I love You and am in awe of how much You love me. Help me to love those You send to me and those to whom You send me.

Thank You for revelation knowledge. I plead the Blood of Jesus over this and every endeavor You direct me to embark upon in the miraculous Name of Jesus, Amen.

Love,

Celia

Celia Wilson

9
Poem
A Chosen Vessel

Over 30 years ago at a K-Mart Store in San Bernardino where I worked as the Portrait Studio Manager one of my customers brought me some poems. This poem was one of them. It speaks to my spirit today as much as it did then. While the author is unknown he/she is blessed and has blessed me. I hope it blesses you.

God Did You Call Me A Toilet?

The Master was searching for a vessel to use.

On the shelf there were many, which one would he choose?

"Take Me", said the gold one,
"I'm shiny and bright,
I'm of great value and I do things just right;
My beauty and luster will outshine the rest,
And for someone like you, Master,
gold would be best!"

The Master passed on with no word at all;

He looked at a silver urn, narrow and tall.

"I'll serve you, Dear Master,

I'll pour your wine;

And I'll be at your table whenever you dine;

My lines are so graceful,

my carvings so true,

And silver will always compliment you."

Celia Wilson

Unheeding the Master passed on to the brass.

It was wide-mouthed, and shallow, and polished like glass.

"Here! Here!" cried the vessel,

"I know I will do, Place me on your table for all men to view."

"Look at me!" called the goblet of crystal so clear,

"My transparency shows my contents so dear,

Thought fragile I am,

I will serve you with pride,

And I'm sure I'll be happy in your house to abide."

The Master came next to a vessel of wood,

Polished and carved it solidly stood,

"You may use me, dear Master",

the wooden bowl said,

"But I'd rather you used me for fruit, not for bread."

God Did You Call Me A Toilet?

Then the Master looked down and saw a vessel of clay,

Empty and broke in it helplessly lay;

No hope had the vessel that the Master might choose,

To cleanse, and make whole,

to fill, and to use...

"Ah!   "This the vessel I've been hoping to find,

I will mend, and use it, and make it all mine."

I need not the vessel with pride in itself;

Nor the one who is narrow to sit on the shelf;

Nor one who is big-mouthed and shallow and loud;

Nor one who displays his contents proud;

Nor the one who thinks he can do all things just right;

But this plain earthly vessel filled with my power and might.

Then gently he lifted the vessel of clay,

Mended, and cleansed it, and filled it that day;

Spoke to it kindly..."There's work you must do...

Celia Wilson

Just pour out to others as I pour into you."

Blogs: godtalksnow@blogspot.com
   trainingqueens@blogspot.com
   theywerearekids@blogspot.com

Email: familyempowermentconsultants@gmail.com
www.familyempowermentconsultants.weebly.com

Books: ANOINTED Married Christian Men
   Looking Through the Eyes of Love (Poetry)
   Overcoming In Christ

Laminated Inspirational Poetic Pocket Cards

Notes

God Did You Call Me A Toilet?